What Readers Are Saying About
WHEN LOVE IS ANGRY

"Great story of real life."

"I couldn't put the book down. I was anxious to get to the conclusion."

"I absolutely love this and may I say, I am personally within a lot of the pages. Every page got more and more intense because of the dialogue between the two authors. It gave me something to look forward to in turning the pages."

"I like the format of hearing from both authors on the same subject or time period. That really worked."

OTHER BOOKS BY RUTH GRIFFIN

After The Call

Full of Grace

Speak Tenderly To Her

Stay With Me

Stepmothers Anonymous

The Book of Joy

WHEN LOVE IS ANGRY

A Memoir From
the Other Side of
Mental Illness

Maurice L. Griffin
Ruth E. Griffin
Foreword by Dr. Andrea L. Hines

Studio Griffin
A Publishing Company
www.studiogriffin.net

When Love is Angry: A Memoir From the Other Side of Mental Illness. Copyright © 2021. Maurice L. Griffin and Ruth E. Griffin

All Rights Reserved. No part of this book may be used or reproduced in any manner whatsoever without written permission except in the case of brief quotations embodied in critical articles and reviews.

For information, contact:
Studio Griffin
A Publishing Company
Garner, North Carolina
studiogriffin@outlook.com
www.studiogriffin.net

Cover Design by Ruth E. Griffin
Images by © gojalia/Adobe and © Benjavisa Ruangvaree/Adobe

Unless otherwise noted, all Scripture quotations are taken from the Holman Christian Standard Bible®, Copyright © 1999, 2000, 2002, 2003, 2009 by Holman Bible Publishers. Used by permission. Holman Christian Standard Bible®, HCSB®, and Holman CSB® are federally registered trademarks of Holman Bible Publishers.

First Edition

ISBN-13: 978-1-954818-22-4

Library of Congress Control Number: 2021936244

1 2 3 4 5 6 7 8 9 10

To all the husbands, fiancés, and any man in a relationship: get quiet and listen. Most of the problems we experience in our relationships today were created because we were too busy talking and simply not listening. And when I say listen, I don't mean when someone is agreeing with you or saying something you like. But when someone is angry, upset or even lashing out at you. Often times we get offended, humiliated, and embarrassed at the emotional words expressed in our direction, but rarely do we take time to look deeper at the anger to find the source of it.

As you read this book, you will see that was the biggest mistake I made. At times, it made me look like a jerk when I thought I was being this great Godly husband. This arrogance could have cost me one of the greatest gifts God gave me (outside of my children, Javin, Jeremiah, Hannah, and Samantha). One thing I realized through this: a gift from God will always be a gift, even if the person receiving it doesn't realize it. You never want a gift given to you rescinded and given to another (and if you've ever had that happen, you know the hurt associated with it).

Men, my hope is that in reading this book, if you are currently living any part of my story, you'll make every effort to start changing yourself immediately. 'Don't be like me, be better than me.' I know it's a commonly used phrase, but I mean every word of it.

Maurice

TABLE OF CONTENTS

Foreword	1
Introduction	5
Storms	9
The Early Years	11
The South	17
The Crack	31
The Meds	35
Frustration	44
Helplessness	55
Bad Actions	71
The Warning	84
Why	95
Purpose	108
More Information	113
Acknowledgements	115
About The Authors	119

WHEN LOVE IS ANGRY

A Memoir From the Other Side of Mental Illness

FOREWORD

It is rare that I have an opportunity to meet a family where every member is talented. Sometimes it is the parents or perhaps the siblings, but I have not often been fortunate enough to enjoy the talent of each family member that I knew. And then several years ago I met the Griffins. Father—talented videographer, Mom—brilliant author and artist, children—each gifted in their own right. I considered them to be a lovely family. I use the word 'lovely' because they were a beautiful, humble, intelligent, soft-spoken family that was also kind and always willing to serve. Yes, I met them at church, so I 'knew' them through ministry obligations but not outside the walls of the house of God. It was only recently that I learned Ruth, whom I can truly now call my friend, had been diagnosed and living with bipolar depression for years.

I always say that everyone has a story.

However, you will only get to hear what that story is if they decide to tell it. Within the pages of this book is the story of Maurice and Ruth revealing their journey through their eyes. They are telling their own story, but this is someone else's story as well.

'When Love is Angry: A Memoir From the Other Side of Mental Illness' is raw and real. You may have a clinical view of different types of mental illness and how to handle the issues surrounding what can often be devastating and debilitating. But within these pages you will read the truth and transparency of a husband and wife as they share their hearts and their love through lenses riddled with pain, misunderstanding and frustration. It is written in the format of an exchange between a husband bold enough to bare his soul and his wife who is determined to productively live with a disease that had taken over her life. Their story takes you to places that are personal and private but necessary to heal broken spots. It is one of courage and triumph and the way it is presented is masterful.

I was honored to be one of the beta readers on this project, so I feel compelled to share another observation. At first glance you may think this book is not for you, because you are not married or have not dealt with mental illness on this level. Well, I am not married and until I met Ruth and got to know her and pieces of her story, I realized I didn't really understand how people were affected on both sides of the issues surrounding mental illness. But 'When Love is Angry' touched me in ways I was not expecting. I came to the realization that what I did understand was pain, hurt, hopelessness, and frustration when being misunderstood, for whatever reason. I could identify with those things and how it felt to love and not have that love returned. Through Maurice and Ruth's story, I remembered purpose can be birthed in painful places and we can overcome what seems impossible.

I'm sure Maurice and Ruth didn't choose to write this memoir because it would be easy, and they had all the answers. They made a decision that it was a story that needed to be told for couples in similar situations to be enlightened, strengthened and encouraged. I think it is so much more. I am thankful to them for putting aside any reservations they may have had in order to share their lives in a way that is poignant in some places and thought provoking in others. I think it will touch more people than they anticipated and will have a positive impact on all who are blessed to read it. I believe anyone can benefit from their message of hope and the knowledge that there is incredible power and peace through the love of God.

Dr. Andrea L. Hines

Author and Inspirational Speaker

INTRODUCTION

My husband, Maurice (or Mo, as I call him), is a self-proclaimed B-/C English student who would tell you that writing is not his thing. So, when he approached me about writing this book, I was surprised. This was quickly followed by shock when he revealed to me that he had written his part already. I had initially imagined helping him edit or publish, but when he said, "No, it's our book," I immediately went from shock to dread. What did he write? What did he say about me? What was I supposed to write?

I was scared.

Then I read the manuscript. My non-writing husband had done a great job expressing himself in written form, revealing to me things he had not done so before. But now it was my turn to write and let me tell you, the dread was paralyzing. This was our story, and I knew it well. I even knew I would write it one day. But I hadn't expected 'one day' to come so soon. You see, the problem wasn't in the story, or in us telling it. No, the problem was in writing it because in order to do that, I had to relive everything I had worked so hard to forget.

I had my first depressive episode at fifteen years of age. I broke down crying for no logical reason, leaving my mom stunned and comforting her second oldest child in an illogical moment. She didn't know something was wrong, and neither did I. I also didn't know it would be the first of many episodes throughout the years. It became something that was just a part of me, and I didn't connect the dots until I was a mother, with young children, pushed to the edge of insanity. My constant companion was anger that often came out in explosive arguments and ill-placed words I would later regret. This, in turn, fueled the shame I felt, and brought my moods down to a level I couldn't control. I would feel down, cry, and not be able to give a reason why. My body hurt, and my outlook was bleak, to the point where death was the only thing I looked forward to. I was thirty years old before I was finally diagnosed with Bipolar II Depression. But that didn't fix my problems. In fact, it was just the start of them, and it did nothing to assuage the shame that was growing every day. Shame for every wrong word, every wrong action, every emotional response, every 'should'a-done', every 'should'a-did'. Shame over what I was, over what I thought I was, over what I thought I wasn't, over what I did, over what I felt I didn't do.

Shame was my constant companion, and this was what my husband was asking me to relive.

The funny part is that I was never upset at him for putting me in that position and that's because I understood what the truth was: everything I'd been through, everything I pushed through wasn't for me, but for someone else. Someone who just got a mental illness diagnosis. Someone who was struggling to get to center. Someone who couldn't see beyond the moment. Someone who didn't know how to find peace in the midst of their chaos. Someone who didn't know how to find hope in the middle of their storm.

I let the book sit for months before I finally picked it back up. But when I did, I was finally able to let go of the excuses, of the shame and bondage that my mental illness brought with it. All because my husband, a man of few words, took the initiative to write heartfelt words I hadn't heard before, allowing me to see me from his standpoint. Because he did that, I was finally able to let the shame die and share our story with you. I hope it does for you what it did for me.

Ruth

STORMS

MAURICE: I heard this in a sermon from the honorable Bishop Joby Brady: "Storms aren't prejudiced, predictable or purposeless."

When two people come together in Holy Matrimony, they come together for many reasons: compassion, finding the true friend they can't live without, the person they trust with everything, etc. The list goes on and on. Never (or rarely) do people come together and say, "Hey, you look like the perfect person to have an unforeseen storm with me that will arise in one or both of our lives. I want to endure this pain, anger, and frustration with you (that may be caused by you)."

I think that's why it is clearly stated in the wedding vows, 'For better or for worse.' The author knew that there would be unforeseen, rough patches. When I married Ruth, I really don't know if I thought about it; or if I would say (and think) some of the things I did about the lady who gave me her life.

RUTH: 'For better or for worse' aren't the words most people focus on when they're saying their wedding vows. For women perhaps more so than with men, it's the idea that we aren't doing life anymore on our own. We now have a partner to share the most intimate parts of ourselves with. We aren't alone, we have someone to love and to be loved by. Someone to take care of and to be taken care of by. To give of ourselves, to create a family with, to be there with us when things go up and down. Again, this isn't the time we think about the 'worse' part, but if the thought does come up, we know that it's covered.

Of course, when you say, "I do," it's hard to imagine what exactly you're committing to. Yes, the goal is together forever, but when life starts happening, that's when you find out exactly what you agreed to.

THE EARLY YEARS

MAURICE: Ruth and I met in my senior year, at a small liberal arts college in the Midwest. The college was in the middle of nowhere. I truly was in the minority category and anyone can tell you when you are in a small group you notice all others who are not like the majority.

The best way to describe Ruth was that she was short, with a lot of hair. She was fair-skinned, but her features led me to believe she had an ethnic background (she is Latino). The biggest characteristic that attracted me to her, though, was her quietness. She had a peaceful presence. And it was a bonus that she had a relationship with Christ.

We both had work-study and worked in the same office, so our paths crossed regularly. Through conversation and interaction on the small campus, we became friends pretty quickly and from there, it slowly grew into a relationship. It would have probably grown faster but I was involved in another romantic relationship that was fizzling out. Once I finished the spring semester, I went home for, while Ruth stayed in school through the summer.

The fall found us back together in a different scenario. I went home to take a summer class to fulfill my credit requirements for a degree. The class finished, and my romantic relationship was over. Due to the lack of work opportunities in my field of study in my hometown, I set my sights on a bigger city with better employment prospects. My brother lived in a city in Ohio, in a duplex where the other side was vacant. The house was in the historic part of town; the building was old, and the vacant side needed some work. The owner was surprised when he found out I was interested in renting it. In his sympathy, he actually let me name the rent price. So, I got it for little to nothing ($100 a month). The only thing in it that worked was the water and it had a cast iron tub, a toilet, and a bathroom sink. I literally was starting from the ground level, but it was mine.

The college where Ruth and I met was no longer a good fit for her and going home was not an option. Needing a fresh start, it made sense for us to become 'roommates' to help her get on her feet. We moved in as friends, but let's be honest, we were more than that. We were there for five years and when we moved south, we shared the same last name; and two little people in our likeness had been added to the family (though I had one more from another relationship during one of Ruth's and I 'friendship' period).

RUTH: It's easy to sum up five years' worth of relationship in a few paragraphs. It bypasses the challenges that you experienced. But it's those highlights that stand out. Mo stood out. I remember meeting him. There weren't sparks, but it was his friendship that eventually changed that. I was seventeen and on my own. So, I appreciated having someone who was centered, logical, and steady. Mostly though, he could put a smile on my face and make me laugh. We talked often and hung out on campus. We became friends and it was that friendship that got me through my first break-up, my lack of academic study habits, lack of social skills and lack of family.

I was an awkward kid. Talented and wanting to experience the world, but socially awkward with no clear direction.

My mom had remarried three or four years earlier and while my stepfather, an older gentleman of Dutch-German descent, provided for us to whatever degree he could, he didn't want me and my siblings in the house. We were a burden I don't think he anticipated or wanted. And the fact that we were ethnic only sealed that deal. For whatever reason, my mom's heritage as Costa Rican was okay in his eyes, but ours as half Puerto Rican wasn't, so one-by-one, we left or were left behind. My older sister was left behind in Virginia when we moved up north. My younger sister would eventually be shipped off to live with my grandfather in Alaska and my brother would choose to return to New Jersey (our home state) to live with our dad, who hadn't been in our lives for years. Me? We moved to Pennsylvania, my stepfather's home state, in my senior year of high school and in an effort to start my own life, I opted to go to college. But I didn't know what school to apply for. And we didn't have the money to pay for the college application, so I wasn't too sure that this was even really an option. I didn't know what I was going to do. Then one day I came across a college application with 'Fee Waived' stamped on it in red ink. I applied with the help of my English teacher and was accepted. I didn't know where the school was and to be honest, I didn't care. Once I was approved for financial aid and graduated high school, I was gone.

While my family situation was far from ideal, I dealt with my life as best as I could. The situation threw me into adulthood way before I was ready to be on my own, and I made lots of mistakes. But I knew, from the moment Mo and I became romantically involved, we were meant to be together. I was sure that God had directed our steps to meet. To this day, I cannot tell you where I got that college application. And after I got it, it was the only school I applied to. But I knew that I knew that I knew we were meant for each other. And that's the belief I carried into our relationship.

So, it seemed like fate that when I was formally disinvited from college (I was kicked out for poor grades) and I couldn't return home (my mother disapproved of Mo because of his skin color and disinherited me when I wouldn't break up with him), I was able to move in with him. I went from being alone to having someone with me, someone for me. We went through some good times, and some rocky times in Ohio. I became pregnant, but miscarried, only to eventually give birth to our son and oldest daughter. We got married and started our lives together as husband and wife. I was sharing my life with my best friend.

THE SOUTH

MAURICE: I started my career in Ohio, and it took us southeast. I had always been in the Midwest, but I visited the south often as a child and really like the weather, friendliness, and slower pace of living. We relocated to a suburb near a growing major metropolitan area. We had the best of both worlds: living out in a rural region where we had space, but only a twenty-minute drive from an active urban area. Life was going along well; I was getting established in my new job. Ruth was raising our two young children while also getting herself established in the work force.

About a year after moving, God decided that the family wasn't quite big enough, and our youngest came along. Life got even busier with three children under the age of ten in a household (and a fourth during the summer months). We were like any other young family—school, daycare, work, church, oh my! Everything seemed to be fine, then came the day where Ruth sat me down and told me she felt like she was going crazy in her mind and that she needed help. If I remember correctly, my oldest son had acted up (as any child does growing up). Ruth said she got so angry with him that she reacted in a way that was unfitting for a mother. She said it felt as though it could have been abuse on her part and this really scared her because what she felt inside could no longer be ignored, controlled, or kept quiet.

In a crisis, I did what most Christians do and turned to God, believing this was a setback we'd work through. That I believe was true; but I was naive about the energy, sacrifice, and strength it would take to walk this out. I was also totally blind to the time involved. This wasn't something that was going to be solved quickly, this was the beginning of at least a fifteen-year journey (and counting).

I started off making a mistake (a few of many as you will read in this book): I was trying to fix something by faith which I truly didn't understand. I didn't fully listen to what Ruth was saying and how she was saying it. My attitude was, if there's a problem, let's fix it and how we fix it is by going to God, he would do the rest.

God was the right foundation, but I was going to him ignorantly. I was going to him with what I thought should be done instead of what Ruth needed. I didn't have the vital information God needed to begin the work. Plus, I wasn't ready. And I didn't think I needed to do anything.

Next mistake: never give your opinion or act in another person's crisis until you take the time to fully understand what the person is dealing with. Get all the information you can before you implement or say anything, even if you already know the answer.

Truth be told, I believe I had noticed things that I thought were normal, but if I looked closer, I probably would have taken it as a clue that something wasn't quite right. Anyone married to a woman knows that through the natural course of the menstrual cycle, changes occur—physically and mentally. These changes can affect moods, thoughts, and actions. I noticed these changes in my wife. She became very opinionated about everything and usually it came with a negative undertone. Not to mention little things would set her off—anything from the kids acting up to someone not agreeing with her opinion would send Ruth from her calm, quiet demeanor, to a fussing outburst in the blink of an eye.

I've never been confrontational. My coping mechanism has always been to stay away and not engage. You can't fuss, fight, or argue when only one person is talking. And this is the point I got to. I would even track her cycle, so I knew when it was time to shut down and stay away (or at least an arm's length). I became so sensitive that if I forgot and noticed wrappers in the bathroom trash, I would tell myself, "Don't engage. It's only a matter of time before an explosion will happen." Then the shutdown would last a good five to seven days.

It says very clearly in the wedding vows, "Let no man separate what God has joined." But by me avoiding Ruth, I was creating something that should never be allowed between a married couple and that is space! Ruth was doing as a lot of women have done (and still are doing), which was dealing with emotional distress on a normal day. Add in a monthly hormonal change, then on top of that the feelings of depression and that is a rough spot to be in.

During this time as Ruth was seeking professional help, I was in the mindset of expecting her and God to work this out. I felt it was something that God could only fix. As I went on with life as the head of the household, I expected Ruth to catch up once God healed her mind. I had no idea it was going in the opposite direction than what I was expecting (and truthfully believing God for).

One thing that the doctor's recommended was Ruth start taking medications. I remember her telling me about that and me strongly voicing my opposition to it. Even today, my thought is, medications may be needed, just proceed very cautiously when taking them for mental illness. There's always side effects, the question is which one(s) will manifest and will it be better or worse than the actual illness?

Ruth started a treatment for her depression. Even with her on medication though, I noticed that I was still avoiding her once a month as I really didn't see any changes. I was still dealing with a very opinionated, pessimistic person during the cycle's times. Really there were times it would carry over. With such a young, growing family taking a lot of our time, it was easy at the end of the day to just go have me-time (which was usually becoming a coach potato in front of the TV) or just going to sleep, as opposed to having any meaningful adult communication time.

RUTH: What should have followed our wedding day was, "...and we lived happily ever after..." That's the fairy tale ending we're conditioned to believe for, but it never happens like that, because this is life. Even before we moved, I was starting to notice mood swings. I thought it was me working out stuff (like my parents' abandonments, my lack of family connection, etc.). And indeed, I knew these were things I needed to work through with God, but I didn't understand the changes that were happening in me.

We moved south; and again, life wasn't what we thought it should be. It certainly wasn't what I expected. I couldn't find a job for three months. I had started my career as a graphic artist at a television station up north. It was a job that I loved, but now I couldn't find anything. And we were having trouble living on one paycheck. I finally had to register with a temp agency, and in my eyes, settle for a job as an administrative assistant. I was nothing more than a secretary with a fancy title. My pride was wounded. There was nothing I wouldn't do for my husband, but I couldn't help the jealousy growing within me—he got to continue working in his career of choice, but I had to give mine up. I never said anything but took my hurt to God. Not to work it out, mind you, but to complain. It wasn't fair. But then, none of what followed was.

I had a job now, but I was basically working to pay childcare. Then our vehicle was repossessed. We fell behind on rent often. We did what we could to eke out the basics. Still, we had to keep living, we had to keep pushing. I was often overwhelmed, but any conversation with Mo was deflected towards God. He didn't have the answers, God did, and he didn't have a problem telling me that. Mo was right. It was just hard to have faith when it was never modeled for me. Yeah, you hear preachers and pastors say, "Have faith," but what does that even mean? How do you do that when there's no money in the bank for diapers? God provided, but in my mind, I was just repeating the cycle of lack I had grown up in and I hated it.

Our youngest was born and that only seemed to add to all the stress. Looking back on it now, I can honestly say I was suffering with postnatal depression, but back then, I didn't understand what I was going through. I was depressed, but I couldn't say that. I was a Christian. I had been taught to have faith that God was the fixer of our problems and if I wasn't seeing our problems fixed, then something was wrong with me. And something was very wrong, just not that. I was afraid all the time, afraid especially of being alone with the kids. My mind was clouded with thoughts of hurting them. I was on eggshells all the time. But at the time, I was also a time bomb, waiting to explode. The little things they did, innocent things, normal things, set me off. I would yell, and then feel horrible. I never hit them when that anger came, but I came close and that scared me. I resented them for being there when my moods were low, and I resented my husband for not being there so that my moods wouldn't get low.

I wanted so desperately to change, but I didn't know how. And I couldn't speak to Mo. Let me rephrase that: I chose not to. I convinced myself that he would only say, "What do you expect me to do?" and then tell me to go to God. But I was going to God. I just wasn't getting a response. I felt like I couldn't hear him, like he was a million, billion miles away. We had our devotion times and that was fine, but when the moods hit and the thoughts clouded my mind and my judgment, I couldn't see beyond my own nose. There was nothing—no future, no hope, no redemption. I was getting worse, and I had no recourse. I had no one.

That was my mindset. I could do amazing things when I focused. I wrote my first book. I started making plans for subsequent books. I started believing that I had a destiny beyond being 'just' a wife, mother, and secretary. I started to see something that resembled hope. But then the moods would hit again, and I would go back to the negative, confrontational, angry person I had become.

I don't remember the incident that set it off, but I remember seeing a commercial for bipolar depression. In it, a woman was yelling and screaming, much like I often did, and then the film froze, capturing her face in a moment of frenzy. Her mouth was open, her eyes were wild, angry, and her face was distorted, ugly. It hit me then. "That's me," I thought. "That's what I look like. That's what my family sees." It wasn't until that moment that I even considered applying a name to this thing I was feeling, a name beyond my own. I had bipolar depression.

I don't remember much of the conversation with my husband, though I do recall telling him I felt like I was going crazy. I remember asking for help, though I don't recollect his response. I remember making an appointment with my family doctor and telling her about my moods. I remember her asking me questions and diagnosing me as bipolar. I remember her prescribing me pills to help with the mood changes and telling me that I was quite lucid for someone in my condition. I remember her encouraging me and telling me that everything would be alright. I also remember taking home the prescription and telling my husband what she said. Any hope

I had when I left my doctor's office was dashed in that moment, when my husband advised that he didn't agree with the medication and insisted I didn't need to take them.

I was so torn. I wanted to be better, but I also needed to have faith in God. And certainly, I couldn't have faith and take medication at the same time … right?

I filled the prescription, but I didn't take the pills. I just carried them with me. I don't know why. I was hoping for something, but I couldn't tell you what.

I started seeing a counselor in addition to my family doctor. Her name was Helen, and she was a sweet, older woman who listened intently as I answered the questions she posed to me, questions about me, my family, and my mental state. She applauded me for seeking help. When she asked about my medication, I remember I pulled out the bottle and set it on the coffee table between us. I explained my crisis of faith and briefly, my husband's hesitation. I don't remember her exact words, but she asked me if I thought that the pills could help me, wouldn't God want me to try them? Then she encouraged me to think about it.

I left that first session still conflicted, but later that night, I decided to take that leap. I don't think I mentioned it to my husband—he had voiced his opposition but left it up to me. I didn't know what to expect as I swallowed that first pill. Part of me wanted a miracle but the truth was I had convinced myself that I wasn't going to get one. I was taking medication; therefore, God wasn't going to fix this. I couldn't articulate it then, but I had lost hope that God could help me. He only did that for other people. I had seen it. My own grandmother had been cured of cancer. But this was something else. Who ever heard of God healing bipolar depression? Who even heard of a Christian *dealing* with bipolar depression? No, I was on my own with this one. My husband didn't agree, didn't want to hear what I was going through, didn't want to deal with my tears. And God? Well, he was too busy with other people to help me. I had no one to talk to, except Helen.

I started seeing her once a month. She recommended books for me to read and gave me assignments that would help me delve into my emotional state to understand who I was and what it meant to be depressed. She was truly a Godsend, but I was still deeply entrenched in the habits I had created, and I didn't understand those were the things I needed to change.

I remember sitting at the kitchen table one time, crying as I worked on one of worksheets. Mo made a comment about it but rather than respond, or even share what I was working on, I dried up my tears and did something else. We were over ten years into our relationship, but early on he had said that he wouldn't talk to me when I cried because I was too emotional to talk rationally. All I heard though was, "I won't talk to you when you cry." So, I started trying to hide my tears. When the depression hit, I would hide in the bathroom and cry. I would cry on the way to work, cry in the bathroom at work, cry on the way home. But I wouldn't cry in front of him. And truthfully, there was a peace about him that rubbed off on me when he got home in the evening, so I wanted to be around him, I needed to be around him. Even though we didn't talk, there was something about him that I yearned for, something that gave me the peace I didn't have.

To be fair, I had been conditioned from a young age to not talk. My mother was a naturalized citizen, but her experience with other people was one filled with discrimination and distrust. We were constantly told not to share with anyone outside of the house what went on in the house. So, I didn't, then and now. And it was killing me.

THE CRACK

MAURICE: One of the things I was encouraged to do during premarital counseling was to make time and create a place for date night. At first, it was fun and exciting. It was a chance to get away from the children and focus on listening to one another. But after a while, I found myself working just as hard to make it happen ... find a babysitter, prepare the kids (making sure they had eaten, bathed, were in their PJ's). Then drop them off, find a spot to eat, go out to the restaurant. Then after that go back get the kids, get home, get them in bed and then finally lie down to rest. Honestly by the time I had some food in me, I was ready to go home and sleep.

The other thing that was taxing was I felt I was the only one planning the evening. I would constantly be asked, "What are we doing or where are we going?" After a while, I asked that question back to Ruth. Sometimes I'd get, "I don't know, what do you want to do?" I believe on a few occasions I got the answer, "You probably won't like what I want to do."

Because I wasn't looking at the big picture (of it being about Ruth; really, of us having space to be us; to talk, listen, and express ourselves openly and honestly in a safe judgement-free space), it soon became less of a priority. We tried to do a weekday evening, but between my mindset and a few second shifts, we'd miss a week here and there. It just became easier to say in my mind, "If Ruth wants to plan something, I'll go, but I ain't doing all the work. It just isn't that fun or useful for me," when deep down it was vitally important.

Another thing I noticed, which I believe helped push me away from date night, is that in giving Ruth the space to talk and vent, we spent a lot of time in what I'll phrase as the 'negative zone.' I believe as humans we all need outlets to rid ourselves of stress, frustrations, bad thoughts, emotions, vibes or however you want to phrase it, that life can bring. I tried to give Ruth that, but it seemed in some cases we never left there, and I sometimes wondered if there was anything nice she could say. I am in no way perfect but if I have a problem, I try to at least come up with a solution. If I don't have one, I'll usually ask for help to find one. I try to end on a positive note. Don't get me wrong I have fallen short many times and God even has (and continues) to show me when I don't meet expectations and standards of someone who would be considered positive. I just got tired of listening to Ruth share the negatives about her work, or what was just as bad, we spent dinner talking about the children. Date night is for the husband and wife, not the kids. In all fairness, Ruth probably got tired of me not talking or complaining about my day at work as well.

Once date night became a side thought for me, stress fractures or small cracks started to appear in our communication. We didn't have a safe space anymore for us to be us and more importantly for us to work on us.

RUTH: The cracks for me were already happening, they were already widening. And I won't blame my husband for them. I wasn't easy to live with. I was negative. I was emotional.

And I had stopped hoping. I was now taking two and a half pills a day but what it was doing, I couldn't tell you. I didn't see a difference. I stopped trying to get better, I stopped trying to do stuff at home. I was functioning, don't get me wrong. If anything, I was still doing that because I had to. But I was doing the barest minimum. And I was always focused on the negative. That's all I saw, everywhere. I hated my job; I hated the people I worked with. I hated the people I commuted with. I hated Mo for having a career while I had to settle for a job that I felt was beneath me. I hated going to church. I hated everything. My anger was boiling over and there was nothing to look forward to. Our lives were routine, and I was racked with guilt over the way I was responding to everyone. The only ones I was open and honest were the kids. I let them know that I was sick, and that I was sorry for yelling so much. But I don't know that I ever said I was trying. Mostly I just apologized.

THE MEDS

MAURICE: Prescription medication for some is necessary, but there are always side effects with taking them. The question then becomes, "Are the side effects less of a cost than the illness?"

I mentioned it earlier: Ruth was on medication, and even began seeing a therapist. In all honesty, I was okay with the therapist. Talking to someone can help you see your life clearly and help you make adjustments when and where needed. But I noticed that 'a' medication became 'medications', and that to me was a little concerning because I remember when Ruth and I talked, my understanding was that it was just an aid to help her as she began to face, get a grip, deal with, and heal from her depression (with no set timetable). To me, it seemed like the meds were becoming the solution to healing the illness.

Ruth was adamant that they were helping, but she was the only one that was seeing that. And I was still behaving the same way before she started taking the meds: avoiding her during certain times of the month. The medication was doing what I feared it would do, which was lie to her, make her think that it was working or working more than it actually was.

Even though we had insurance and small co-pays, when you're filling multiple prescriptions multiple times a year, all of that adds up. At the time, we had a young, growing family, and every cent was accounted for. This rising cost (no matter how small) wasn't part of our budget. I don't like to waste money, and to me I often wondered, "How much of these medications are really necessary?"

One thing I did notice about her taking the medications was that they put her in extreme moods. Sometimes she would be happy-go-lucky and then other times she would be negative and sarcastic (which is what I considered normal or what I was used to). Sometimes it would switch daily. I also noticed sometimes it seemed like she was in a mental fog. I would tell her important household or husband-wife matters and a few days later if it came up in conversation, Ruth would be adamant that it was the first time I told her. When I disagreed and went back to the previous time I mentioned it, I would be greeted with a hostile opposition at which point, I'd simply drop the conversation, because I wanted peace and we weren't getting anywhere.

There were so many times I wanted to say that I didn't notice any difference in her medication, but I kept my mouth shut because I knew it would end in both of us on opposite ends and unwilling to budge. Finally, I made what I thought was an extra effort to mention things to Ruth. I was met with, "You should be glad that I'm taking this because I would be worse if I didn't."

I felt helpless. I felt the medication was more important than my opinion or God in her life. Along with the feeling of helplessness, in some ways I felt we were stuck. At this point, I knew only God could break through our stalemate. In this sobering moment I begin to share my concerns about my wife to God.

I really can't say too much about the therapy, Ruth did share some. I'm not sure what all was said during that time, so it's hard for me to say if she took full advantage of everything her therapist shared. My issue was only with the medications and what I deemed was the increased amounts.

RUTH: After some time, I started showing serious side-effects of the first drug I was placed on. My doctor advised me to stop taking it immediately and make an appointment to see her. That was a Friday. The appointment wasn't until Monday, and because the medication was so strong, I went into withdrawal. I was sick, I couldn't stop shaking, I wanted to die. Mind you, I wasn't suicidal nor was I experiencing death ideation at that point. The pain was just so bad, it was all I could think to do to make it stop.

That Monday, I was placed on another medication. After about a month, that one failed me too. Another medication followed. It was $80 a month, after the insurance was applied. I couldn't justify that on our budget. I didn't even tell my husband, I just asked for another medication. But the next one put me to sleep for two days. I actually missed work because I slept through my day.

When all was said and done, I would work my way through seven medications until I finally found one that helped.

At that point, my family doctor referred me to a psychiatrist, who was better equipped to help me. Helen recommended that I end my sessions with her and just see the psychiatrist only. She wrote me a letter of introduction for the doctor, sharing with him what she had diagnosed me with (bipolar depression with OCD tendencies) and how she had helped me. I showed it to my husband, but he adamantly declared I wasn't OCD and wouldn't talk about it any further. I learned then I couldn't talk to him about my treatment.

I started seeing the new doctor. He took the letter, said nothing about it and then asked me questions. I answered them, but I couldn't shake the vibe that I was on an assembly line and he was just trying to get through the appointment. He wrote me a prescription for the one medication that ended up working;

and it was a Godsend in more than one way—I didn't experience any side-effects and it was only $5. At the very least, I wouldn't have to feel guilty about breaking our budget.

All-in-all, the appointment lasted ten minutes and I left feeling cheated. This certainly wasn't what you saw in movies. But he was my doctor now, there was nothing I could do. I didn't know I could ask for another doctor, I didn't know I could interview them the same way they interview us. I just went with it. What was the point anyway? The first thing he told me was that there was no cure for bipolar depression, no miracle pill that would take the symptoms away and I had to learn how to live with it. His words were what I walked away with and whatever hope I had left began dying.

But I was still trying. I had the worksheets Helen gave me and I would look them over. I wrote in my journal every day. I conversed with God in them. I did most of the talking, but I like to think he listened. I started researching my condition and discovered I wasn't alone—there was a community of bloggers who shared their pain in blog form. I was astounded that people out there spoke about their issues freely (as opposed to the silence in the church) and viewed myself as part of them. I started my own blog and chronicled my feelings and recapped my appointments with my doctor. I kept it anonymous, as I hadn't told anyone (family, friend, or church members) of my diagnosis. But then my husband commented negatively on one of my posts—I had said something about my doctor, and he told me that by talking about him like that, I was giving off a negative impression. I said nothing and stopped blogging.

I think my hope was dead by then. It wasn't any one person, or any one thing, but a combination of everything. Why should I try? What was the point of even trying? If I could just keep doing what I was doing, then at the very least, I could keep functioning, if only for the sake of the kids. I didn't realize that even though I hid my tears, I couldn't hide the negativity, the outbursts, or the anger. I tried, but they always found a way through.

With my hope gone, I entered a new phase of the disease—I started idealizing death. I remember asking my doctor after our usual ten-minute appointment to explain the difference between the ideation and suicidal thoughts. He told me that suicide was actively seeking death, while the ideation was just thoughts. He didn't express too much concern after I told him I wasn't suicidal. He asked about it maybe once or twice after that, but it was never the focal point of any appointment. And I certainly didn't tell Mo because I didn't want a repeat of the first and only time I shared with him what it felt like to want death.

My first pregnancy (in 1994) ended in a miscarriage. Neither one of us was ready to be parents, but when I started bleeding twelve weeks in, I was devastated. A week passed, my doctor announced no heartbeat could be found and I was immediately scheduled for surgery. I was somber when Mo took me to the hospital; non-conversational with the kind nurse who only wanted to make me smile. And when I woke up after the surgery, the first emotion I felt was disappointment—not that I lost the baby, but that I had woken up at all.

The drive home was quiet and painful, but I couldn't shake that feeling of wanting to be dead for a few days. I never mentioned it to Mo, until years later, when I was trying to make him understand the frame of mind I was in. His response was to rebuke the devil for suicidal thoughts, as he walked away from me. To be fair, I sprung it on him, but at the time, I didn't know how to broach the subject at all. And after that experience, I didn't feel like being rebuffed, so I didn't mention it again. I knew to even consider suicide was to sentence my children to a fate that included a higher rate of suicide for them[1], so I resolved early on that I could never kill myself. But with the lack of communication between Mo and myself, I started to believe that if something did happen to me, Mo wouldn't miss me.

---

[1] Children Who Lose a Parent to Suicide More Likely to Die the Same Way.
https://www.hopkinsmedicine.org/news/media/releases/children_who_lose_a_parent_to_suicide_more_likely_to_die_the_same_way. April 21, 2010

FRUSTRATION

MAURICE: When frustration occurs, we can easily fall into the trap of finger-pointing and fault-finding. I was no different, even though I thought it was right.

My job required me to drive to various locations, so I spent a lot of my workday in the work vehicle. During those times, I would talk to God about Ruth. I felt hopeless because I was reliving all the times we would disagree and some of the excuses I thought she would make to me. Often times when Ruth and I would have a conversation of a strong nature, if I brought up something that I felt Ruth needed to change or improve, I was immediately met with, "Well, you do this," so instead of listening to one another and improving ourselves, we were fault finding.

I'm the type of person who likes to analyze situations before speaking, even if I know what I first feel is right. In the case of Ruth, I always held my tongue whenever I noticed something that needed improving. This stems from words God spoke to me when Ruth and I first moved to the south (after only having been married about a year and a half). I remember getting dressed for work one day and the sovereign God showed up and spoke these words: "I HAVE A SPECIAL COVENANT WITH THIS WOMAN AND YOU BETTER HONOR IT."

The funny thing was, at that point, Ruth and I were totally fine in our relationship (or at least, at a peaceful moment). But because of that, whenever something was not in sync as I thought it should have been with her, I usually held my tongue and sat on it, analyzing it before I approached her.

Shortly after that, I remember Ruth approached me and said something that I didn't like. I was getting ready to share my thoughts with her in a very direct manner. I remember looking at her but the only thing that came out of my mouth was, 'Okay.' Even after two plus decades of being together, I still hold my tongue and thoughts until I have a plan of how to proceed (even if she is wrong, I'm never reactionary to her).

So, in these times in the car, I'd pretend Ruth was there. At first, I would act off of something that had happened in the past and use that as a jumping off point to tell her how I felt. I would often say things to point out her negativity and pessimism. How she said very little to build, uplift or find positive in people or situations. How if I mentioned something that seemed out of alignment, she would literally talk for ten minutes on all the things wrong with them or the situation.

When it came to us, if I said something to her that I thought she needed to correct or improve, I wasn't saying it to be mean, I was saying it to help. And sometimes helping is telling people what they may not want to hear but need to. I didn't say this, but she was my wife and I loved her and if I truly loved her as a man of God, part of my responsibility was to cover her. Which meant making sure she was at her best or in the best position to succeed. That may include exposing (and or dealing with) shortcomings in a private setting (which should go both ways in a marriage).

One of the things we seemed to go round and round about was food choices. Ruth enjoyed cuisines that had onions and/or garlic in them. Eating food containing those ingredients when you don't have any mouth fresheners (mints, gum, etc.) can leave a person 'aromatic'. On top of that, I have a sensitive nose. This made close conversations less than optimal. Sometimes the aroma would be so strong that I could smell it outside of normal personal space. Just trying to find a way to approach a sensitive subject like this was hard. I did sit on my comments and tried to come up with a diplomatic way to have this dialogue. I knew something had to be done when I would get home after not seeing my wife all day, and my first thought would be to wonder what she ate and if I had to deal with the aroma of that, or worse, to just hold my breath until I was far enough away to hopefully not smell it.

When I realized that was my first thought, I finally had to say something to her. Not sure what response I'd get, I must say I was a little disheartened by her reply. What should have been just as concerning to me is the fact I was not surprised by her answers. Her reply was either, "I didn't eat anything with garlic." or

"You consume garlic too, but I still hang around you."

To the first comment, I would often ask what she ate, and she would tell me. I would inquire about the seasonings used in the dish. She would often say it had maybe one or no onions; and no garlic was added. I would then ask about the seasonings (side note: I'm kind of a simple foodie. I pay more attention than the average person to how foods are seasoned as well as what's in the seasonings). On further inspection of the seasoning, they usually had one or both forms of onion and garlic.

To her second reply, I do take garlic for medicinal purpose, but I make sure that I immediately brush my teeth, tongue, and anything else to try to get rid of that smell. In the event I'm out and I feel that I might still have the smell (which I have noticed on myself), I truly try to avoid any kind of close quarters with anyone. I'm sure it doesn't work all the time but I'm aware and do make an effort to try to eliminate the smell.

In her frustration, Ruth would say because of my sensitive nose she couldn't enjoy foods she liked to eat. But in my mindset, I wasn't just thinking about me, I was thinking on a larger platform. I would try to explain to her that you can eat those things, just be mindful that you are going to be dealing with people in professional settings from time-to-time. "You have to have something to help combat those aromas. Have mints or gum if you can't brush your teeth and tongue." I go back to the old shampoo commercial slogan, "You never get a second chance to make a first impression." We live in a society where people would soon either not tell you about your flaw or talk about you to others about that flaw rather than help you correct it. I didn't want that for my wife.

But even though I tried to explain it that way, it fell on deaf ears. To be honest, I sometimes did approach her in a confrontational way (or not at the best time), and when someone feels attacked usually their first reaction is to defend themselves or attack back. Even though I thought I was helping, the opposite effect was occurring. This is just one example of how I felt we could not have open conversations about subjects or situations we did not see eye-to-eye on.

RUTH: One thing I learned along the way was that bipolar amplifies what's already in you. As much as we talk about it being a mood disorder, in my experience, it only takes what's in you and makes it seem a thousand times worse. I am an emotional person. You could say that's because I'm Latina, but the truth is, that's just who I am, who I've always been. I think emotionally. I respond emotionally. Emotions aren't bad, they're necessary, they're signals for things we're feeling, things we need to feel. They help us cope with situations and let us know when things are right or wrong. The anxiety we feel when something happens lets us know that we should be leery of the situation because something may be wrong. Fear prepares us to fight or flight. Sadness lets us know that we need people. Happy? That we're in a time for celebration. Our emotions are a gift.

But not when they are unbalanced. And not when we don't know what to do with them. The proper response to anxiety is not to keep being anxious. The proper response to fear is not to live in that state. The proper response to sadness is not to wallow in it alone.

Of course, I didn't know any of that back then. I didn't know anything about myself or how I was supposed to deal with this disease. My rational side went on vacation and left my emotions in charge. And whether it was right or wrong, I just let myself feel whatever my mind was throwing at me.

I continued going to my psychiatrist once a month, but again, we weren't delving into much of anything.

Did I spend money? This is a major symptom for those suffering with bipolar depression; it signals impulsive decisions, which is an indicator for manic episodes. No, I told him. But I wasn't being honest. I would eventually run up a $16,000 debt with a credit card I opened up in my name without my husband's knowledge. I would go shopping on days I was depressed, hoping to feel better, then I would try to hide my purchases. Also, I would eat, because that was the one thing I could shop for and not bring home the evidence of. I spoiled the kids, and then added, "Don't tell dad." I was the 'fun parent.' But when my doctor asked, my answer was often no.

Did I have any emotional outbursts? Sometimes. And I would recount them in tears because I felt guilty, and I had no one else to cry to.

Was I taking my medication? Sure. In fact, I was now not just on an anti-psychotic drug, but also an anti-depressant.

Was I journaling? Yes.

Looking back on it now, I can't recall anything life-changing about my time with this particular doctor, unlike my time with Helen, but that's also because I wasn't doing my part. I wasn't being completely honest, with him or myself. I didn't understand the purpose of the medication, or the appointments, apart from knowing I had to be monitored on them and get screened periodically, because prolonged exposure to them was known to cause kidney damage.

Great, something else to add to the list.

I didn't understand that the drugs were to help bring me to center, to help me level my moods as much as possible so that I could then examine myself and see where I could improve my responses. But because I wasn't responding to the doctor, he couldn't help me the way I needed to be helped.

Then he quit—not just me but the practice. He handed me off to another doctor with a goodbye and good luck; and while the new doctor was more personable, I still wasn't responding to treatment. I didn't care anymore. I was stuck with this disease and there was nothing I could do about it. I let myself respond with what was in me.

My husband said something I didn't like? I responded with, "Well, what about you?"

He critiqued something about me? I fired back with acrid tone.

Someone at work got on my nerves? I cried in the bathroom and came home and complained angrily that life was unfair.

Anger was now my bedfellow and unfortunately, there was no room for all of us in bed. My husband started falling asleep on the couch. I would stay up with him, hoping to keep him awake long enough to get him to come to bed, but I would end up tired. And when I begged him to come to bed, he wouldn't tell me why he didn't want to. I knew it was me, I knew there was something wrong with me, but all I could do was cry myself to sleep.

I would teeter between feeling like I was the worst person in the world and feeling entitled because I did so much for my family, even with my handicap only to get criticized. I hated it when Mo would 'encourage' me to not eat aromatic foods. I understood he was trying to be helpful, but the few words he spoke were received as harsh and uncaring. His intent may have been right, but his delivery was wrong and after a while, rather than explain why, he simply said, "You stink." And I was supposed to receive that as helpful? I got offended that I offended his senses and argued back. But at the same time, I felt like I was losing him, so I gave up what I loved to please what I viewed as his hang-up. I could add martyr to my list of accomplishments, but it wasn't helping me or my marriage.

HELPLESSNESS

MAURICE: Undealt-with frustration can (and more times than not, will) lead to helplessness. When you feel you can't have a real conversation with the person you've pledge your life to, it can leave you with a feeling of despair. This was me and I found even though I thought I was sharing my concerns with God, I was simply just fussing about my wife to him.

Another mistake I made along the way was that I should have at least sought someone with wisdom to talk to. I would sometimes act how I would share my frustrations with my spiritual leader. Then the male machoism would kick in, and I'd say things like, "I know God for myself, he talks to me." I would tell myself that they were too busy, and I honestly felt that this is something Ruth and I could work through (or should try to work through first).

I'll pause right here and say this is one of my shortcomings, trying to seem like I can work out anything with God. This is true, but sometimes God works out situations by sending people or giving you resources in your community. The key is you, or in this case me, having to access those resources.

The other thing I must be honest about is that I'm pretty friendly and engaging but trust is a different issue. I believe everyone needs a true friend, a person who loves you as you are, who is loyal enough to protect your shortcomings, but also honest enough to let you know when you are wrong or need help. The truth is I needed to work at not only trying to be that person but also looking to allow someone to be that in my life, which I wasn't doing.

In the weekly rant sessions I was having with God, little did I know, what I thought was me working out our issues or having a therapy session with him was slowly building resentment towards my wife. I would often talk about how she had a pessimistic attitude and a glass half-empty mentality. It was simply building a larger crack in the foundation of our marriage. I found myself engaging less and less in conversation whenever we were together. It became easier to just shut down when I felt she said something I deemed as negative. Never did I once ask or seek out to understand why she felt the way she did.

In one of my so-called 'God therapy' sessions, as I was talking, I just blurted out, 'I don't really like talking to my wife.' I felt I could not have a serious talk with her, because it usually turned into a tit-for-tat type of conversation and if I felt strong enough to stand on something, I usually ended up with tears from her. Sometimes that would last for more than the moment, with me just getting quiet. In the event I was right, I would get an apology later with an attempt to do better. Frankly, I was tired of that and I felt a lot of our 'serious' talks did not require all of that emotion. I just wanted her to listen, process, and learn from whatever we were talking about, make the change and move forward. I really didn't expect a 180-degree turn but at least some sort of effort to change.

What really was an irritation to me is when I felt I had to express myself on the same issue again. I thought I was giving her time to adjust and correct, but it felt like my words fell on deaf ears. From this and her negative outlook, I simply was tired of going around the same mountain on the same stuff. In that frustration, I think I did the first smart thing in a long time: I realized this had been going on for some years and it was no better. I knew I was not going to fix this so I simply asked God to help Ruth, to help me, to help us because I knew I couldn't change it.

Sometimes between a prayer and the answer is a process, or in my case, a wilderness walk. I began to look back on situations and remember times that Ruth and I were physically away from each other (traveling for work or going to see family), and how I found peace and looked forward to it. Ruth had (over the years) gained some weight. She developed a louder-than-normal breathing pattern when she slept, often times waking me up multiple times during the night. I would sometimes have to retreat to the couch for any hope of rest. It got so serious that if she went to bed before me and I heard her from the living room, I would stay on the couch.

I would quietly walk to our bathroom so as not to wake her and not have to face the questions of when I was coming to bed. The most difficult was when I was already in bed and her loud breathing would start. Whenever I would tell her about it, I would get the reply, "There's nothing I could do." I knew what the problem was—her weight gain—but I knew telling her would only make things worse.

I finally couldn't be quiet about it anymore. Whenever the subject came up, I would tell her she never breathed like that when we were first together, trying to sensitively mention her weight. I can honestly say that I'm not sure how that was received. It got so bad that one time I remember her saying she was going to see her doctor about it. I inquired about her upcoming doctor visit, got the information (date, doctor's name), actually took video of her loud breathing, and sent it to her doctor expressing my concern for her health. It did not change anything right away, so I simply went into shut down mode. I just remember coming home after work and simply getting quiet and staying quiet.

RUTH: I can't tell you when it happened but change for me started after we got a new pastor. He preached a message called, Dream Again. And I'd love to tell you about the message and how deep it was, but I can't. I cannot tell you anything about it because all I heard was the title. It sparked something in me and reminded me that I had stopped dreaming, stopped living, stopped hoping. But as much as that word sparked life back into me, I still had no idea how to live with this thing called bipolar depression. I knew I needed to start dreaming again, but I didn't know how. So, I just kept doing what I was doing.

My depression felt like it was getting worse, so I went back to my doctor, who tried switching me to a new medication. The side effects were terrible, so she put me on another one. The side effects were even worse. She gave me a third one—I didn't even try it. I brought the samples back to her and asked her to put me back on the original medication. She did and added a third pill—a half one actually.

There were a couple of times when it got so bad and I couldn't stop the downward spiral of emotion, that I called my husband and told him I needed help, I needed prayer, I needed something. I could hear the hesitation in his voice, but he prayed for me. And I calmed down. But I couldn't rely on that because the depression would return, and he would ask why I was still dealing with it, why I couldn't trust God, believe him for my healing. I couldn't tell him that I didn't believe God could do that for me. So, I stopped calling him, not wanting to hear that.

My doctor recommended I start keeping a mood chart. I downloaded one I found on the internet and tried to fill it out, but I had no consistency in that area and soon let it fall to the side. I stopped journaling, stopped talking to God. Again, this was me knowing that I needed to start dreaming again.

Instead, I ate. I just let myself feel full, feel satisfied, feel something other than the depression. I had gained weight, but I never weighed myself, never really looked at myself, never realized that I was now eighty pounds heavier than when I started this journey. I didn't realize this until I visited my sister for her son's graduation. I dressed nice, did my make-up, put on jewelry, the whole nine yards. But then I saw the photos from that event, and I was shocked—I looked so big. When did that happen? I was not aware of my eating habits, only that I was never satisfied. I was not aware that it was affecting everything else in my life. I couldn't sleep well, I now snored. I was always tired, always down. I couldn't get enough energy to go to the gym, even though I had a membership. Everyone, including my husband, kept telling me it would help, but what did they know? They weren't the ones suffering with bipolar. They didn't understand. I now felt entitled to my depression, I protected it. It was mine, a part of me. I began to see it as part of my identity, and it was strangely comforting. It was familiar. It accepted me. I embraced bipolar because it was all I had. The kids were getting older, they didn't need me as much anymore; my husband was distant from me. The few friends I had I kept at arm's length so they wouldn't know. That left me with the depression, with the fantasies of having a breakdown and being taken to a hospital, then people would see I was suffering, and I could stop hiding.

You have to understand, I was/am high functioning. Outwardly, I was doing (mostly) what I needed to do. I was getting stuff done. I was writing books. I was working full time. I was taking care of the kids. But inside, I was dying. My life was slowly being drained from me simply because I was holding onto this.

Now mind you, this is not the same as accepting my diagnosis, accepting that I had bipolar depression. That's partly why I struggled for so long. My experience in church had convinced me that to be Christian and bipolar meant that I couldn't even say I was bipolar because then I was speaking something over myself and bringing it into fruition. Not being able to speak about it denied the reality of a disease that was as real as cancer and diabetes, and in the same need of medical treatment. And because I didn't understand this, I resigned myself to it. I embraced it, held onto it, felt entitled to the attention it gave me.

Meanwhile, it pulled me in deeper into the hole it created. With no outlet, I just kept on slipping in further.

But I was supposed to be dreaming and there was a dream that God put on my heart years before I was diagnosed. A big dream.

As a child, art was my passion. I loved drawing, loved coloring, loved painting. It all came naturally to me. And I remember telling God, at the age of about eight years old, that my talent was his. That I would dedicate it to him and serve him however he wanted me to. When I got older, I discovered creative writing. I was in middle school and using that medium more and more for classwork. I had always been a daydreamer, often getting in trouble for staring out of the window, or not paying attention, but now I was creating stories in my head, scribbling down dialogue or scenes in between the teacher's lessons, and then hiding it away in my notebook, to look at it later. I still loved art, I still drew every day, still planned to study art in college, but I found joy in writing.

I enjoyed reading different genres—Gothic horror, romance, classics, mysteries, adventures, etc., and all this influenced what I wrote. I didn't share this with anyone, but often wondered if I was old enough to write, if I was old enough to write adult parts, if I understood that world enough to write it. I started working on my first screenplay ('Beowulf'—I'm a history buff as well) and would rewrite storylines with my younger sister for some of the shows we watched. I didn't understand this was my dream, this was my destiny.

But then life happened, and I let it all go. I stopped writing and just focused on surviving.

I started journaling in 1995 after my miscarriage and started breathing life back into that dream. But I didn't know what it was, didn't know that I should be seeking it, doing it more, developing the gift that had been placed in me. Instead, I finished up art school, got a job in television doing the graphics for a nightly cable news show, and felt fulfilled. I loved it and I was sure I had found my destiny.

Then we moved and all I could find was a temp position.

Hindsight is 20/20 and sometimes when you look back, you see God working in the midst of your pain to get you where you need to be.

For me, that was back to writing. I never understood why I couldn't find a job in graphic design or television, though I had the education and the experience. I always looked at the temp position as a step down, a career I never asked for, never intended to have. But I also never imagined it as part of my destiny. It was, though. It was part of a dream and I had to search God, seek his face to discover that.

That and more. In my time with God, he gave me the words that would eventually become my first book and that sparked a hunger in me to write. I now had idea after idea for Christian books. But also, romances, dramas, comedies, and Biblical Fiction. Especially Biblical Fiction. I wanted to tell the stories found in the Bible from a new perspective, one that stayed true to not just the Bible, but other historical sources. To give readers an opportunity to fall in love with those stories the way I did.

Writing wasn't just a hobby, or a pastime, it was my dream, it was my destiny, and I had to remember that. I had to dream again because I had work to do.

And dream again I did. I had grown tired of being tired; tired of hurting; tired of fighting; tired of being angry. My youngest was now a teenager and the realization that I would soon be alone in the house with Mo was starting to dawn on me. I was scared—we barely talked now, what was going to happen to us then? I had to change.

I started investing more of myself into my appointments with my psychiatrist. The appointments were still only ten minutes, if that, and she basically only asked me questions about how my moods were. I was honest with her though, whereas I wasn't with my previous doctor—but the ideation was now worse. Whenever something didn't go as intended, whenever the depression hit, whenever I felt bad, or ashamed, I now imagined myself cutting open my wrist. I didn't linger on the thoughts, but they were there. I knew they were there. And they knew that I knew. I wasn't actively suicidal, so my doctor wasn't concerned, but she also understood where it could lead, and she made it a point to talk to me about my moods and my thoughts. And about journaling.

I started journaling again, which meant I was now talking to God again. And I was actively trying to understand this disease. It didn't change my responses, because at that point, they were habit. I had conditioned myself to respond to Mo in certain ways, and I could only excuse it, because I still felt powerless to change it, still hopeless, even with this glimmer of hope coming into my life. If there was any change happening, it wasn't showing yet.

I started making goals in 2014. There weren't many of them, and I was struggling with achieving them, but I was making goals—for my writing, and the business of writing, but also for my personal well-being. On top of that list were four specific ones:

1. Keep track of my moods.
2. Take all medication daily.
3. Exercise consistently.
4. Remember that God still heals.

I can't say I believed in the last one, but I desperately wanted to. It seemed out of my scope of ability and I didn't know how to do it, so I focused on the other ones. I had no consistency, but they remained on the list and I tried whenever I could.

It had been nine years since my diagnosis and the dream was slowly coming to life again. It was on life support, but still breathing. I started making changes to my diet and lost some weight. I had peaked at 216 pounds, which for a petite woman, is obese, but now I had dropped to under 200 and while the progress wasn't visible, it was something.

In 2015, my novel, 'Speak Tenderly To Her', placed first in the Latino Literacy Now Books Into Movies contest in the Romance category. The prize was to have the book presented to film producers. There was no guarantee that any of them would contact me, but it was an opportunity. I prepared the query and the spec sheet and mailed ten copies of the book to the organization.

In 2016, one producer contacted me. She loved the book and wanted to offer me an options contract. In exchange, I would agree to give them 18-24 months to find a buyer to the rights for the story. We found an entertainment lawyer, went over the contract and signed it. Then we waited. I was excited, but that excitement waned when I talked to my husband. He told me, point-blankly, "Honestly, I'm praying that God withhold that opportunity from you until you're ready. What if you get it? You're not fit, you're overweight. You don't have the stamina for this. That's my prayer."

I was hurt. I told him I was trying, that I had changed my diet, that I was walking now, but he argued if I was really trying, there would be more results. I needed to put more efforts into it. I let his words affect me like they always did but I didn't give up. Those days were done.

BAD ACTIONS

MAURICE: This really started when an issue was discovered in Ruth's body and a fairly common surgery was required. I took time off work to be with her and to make sure she was okay. I remember my mother having this same procedure and how the weeks after the surgery went in our household (not good). All I could say (which I am in no way proud of) is that I made up my mind that once Ruth was home and okay, I was not going to be anywhere near her. I was thinking of all kinds of things to get done that I had been putting off.

I remember on the day of the surgery, I was in the waiting room, fighting an internal battle. I prayed for her and felt she was going to be okay, but all I could think about was going to the gym and getting my workout in. Then the other thought was, "I'm going to be able to get a peaceful night sleep at home in my bed." I asked God, "What the hell is wrong with me?"

Ruth came through the surgery well and was in recovery for a few hours (while the anesthesia wore off). During that time, I stepped away and ran to the gym. I remember vividly being on the treadmill, battling in my mind and saying to myself. "This is for my health," but also having that thought, "Maurice, should you really be here now?"

After the gym, I went back to the hospital. By this time, Ruth was awake and in her room. I sat quietly, working on a work project to pass the time. I kept fighting off the feeling of being excited to just be alone in a quiet house. After a few hours, I asked Ruth if she was okay. She said she was, and I left. I strangely felt relief when I got home, but also still battled the thoughts that I shouldn't be feeling that way when my wife was in the hospital. Something was wrong,

I wasn't a totally awful person. I like to cook and do most of the cooking in our household. So, thinking ahead I wanted to make sure Ruth at least had something to eat when she got home. I made her a large pot of vegetable soup that night and relaxed the rest of the evening. The next day Ruth was discharged, and I went to pick her up. Once she got home and situated, I was off to the gym. As time went on, I simply became more and more quieter at home. Ruth's body healed and she went back to work. But I can remember evenings where I came home and sat in my work truck, wondering why I didn't like talking to my wife.

I can remember her telling me about her day and me just listening and thinking to myself, "Why is she so negative? I have problems at work too, but I leave them there. I don't want to give any of them my personal time, why should she?" The more she talked, the quieter I got. I believe she noticed, because there were a few times she would ask me if I was okay. I'd say I was fine which was not the case because when you don't want to talk to your wife, something is wrong! And church was a glaring reminder of that.

I volunteer in our media ministry at church, doing camera work. I am usually positioned in the corner of the stage, gathering crowd shots for our live production. The Bishop would sometimes mention his love for his wife and family. I would talk to God then and say, "Help me, Lord, because I really don't like talking to my wife." I should have been agreeing with him, instead I was crying out to the Lord on the inside for help.

If there was a saving grace in all of this, it would be that I knew there was a problem and even in my own complaining about Ruth, I was talking straight to God because I knew he was the only one who could help. I'm a thinker and like to think I believe I am observant. During this time, I noticed she was yelling a lot more. To be fair, we had teenagers at home and any parent knows that teens can sometimes test every last patient cell you have in your body. So, they did stuff, but there were times when I felt it was a small thing that maybe needed correcting, but we were all subjected to Ruth's anger outburst. It got so bad sometimes I would have to interject and ask her, "Why are you yelling?" She would often blame the kids and then switch to, "You married me." I would reply, "Back then you were quieter and didn't scream." She would comeback with how bad it was back then internally, and this was better to what was going on then.

This was the type of dialogue we had. All this did was push me away so when she did talk, I'd only answer when it was necessary (short answers when 'yes' or 'no' wasn't enough). I think as my God car sessions went on, I would continue to complain about Ruth. I don't know if I got tired of it or simply had no other recourse. So instead of complaining to God, I began to practice how I would tell her exactly how I felt. As I talked things out, I would share how she was very black and white in her thoughts and opinions; and not really open to another school of thought; how I felt she was unforgiving. I really started to believe if I betrayed her trust (and I don't mean infidelity) that I would probably have to leave because I felt I'd never be forgiven.

If you notice, that small crack in our marriage had become wider. I was noticing it too. This was concerning to me because I had heard of people splitting up and it usually started with issues like this that were ignored or never worked on. I had (or have) no intentions of this. I also had heard divorced people say they had no intentions of splitting up either. I can honestly say the 'D' word (divorce) was never, ever an option. But things had to change.

One day, during one of my vehicle practice talks, I came to the conclusion Ruth was angry. I really believed she was, but the real question for me was WHY and/or WHO was she angry with (which could have included me)?

Even with that knowledge though, I still didn't make an effort to tell her how I felt. I was feeling that nudge that I should, especially if I wanted to see things get better, but I didn't yet.

RUTH: In addition to the depression, I started cramping outside of my regular period and my flow became heavier. My family doctor referred me to an OBGYN who diagnosed me with adenomyosis. Surgery was scheduled—a partial hysterectomy—but I also feared what that meant for us. My mother-in-law had had a similar procedure well before I met her, but I only remembered my husband talking about how he never wanted to be around her during that time because of the mood swings. I knew if I had the surgery, he would pull further away from me. But I was looking forward to it, if only to get relief from the cramps and never have another period again (a silver lining in an otherwise bleak life).

I remember calling Mo the day I left my doctor's office and advising him of the surgery date. Our conversation was brief, but it was memorable for this reason—it was the last time he spoke to me for the better part of a year. There were the quick responses (yes, no), but no conversation beyond that. I thought perhaps I was reading into his moods, especially when he would respond in the positive when I asked if he was okay. But the breaking point came one day about a month later when I discovered our eldest daughter had gone out of town to visit a crush and lied about it. She was eighteen at the time, so technically she was an adult, but she was still living under our roof. I called Mo to share this with him, but he didn't answer his phone. This was after work hours, so I called him again, but again, he didn't answer. I called a couple more times, but I still got the same response—nothing. I finally left him a message and asked him…no, begged him to call me back. He never did.

I was broken at that point. I had arrived at the parking lot of our local gym, but I was in tears and hysterics. I didn't know what to do. I didn't know how to get him to respond to me. All I could think to do was to call my older sister. She answered on the first or second ring (which was a miracle in itself—she's not very good at keeping track of her cell phone) and then she patiently listened as I poured out my heart.

In hindsight. I genuinely believe if she hadn't answered the phone that night, my marriage, and my life, might have been over. Again, those thoughts came, the death ideation, to the degree that my wrist actually started hurting and my heart FELT like it had physically broken. But my sister was wise enough to start with a prayer before she gave me any advice. We spent an hour on the phone, with her sharing her heart, God's word, and an unbiased perspective. I never made it inside the gym that night but was able to dry up my tears enough so that I could drive home. She encouraged me to not talk back, argue or confront; to be careful about using trigger words, as she put it, that Mo could view as an attack on his ego, because then I was just setting us up for an argument. Lastly, but most importantly, she advised me to pray for Mo. It all sounds simple, but it sure didn't feel like it when he finally got home. He said nothing and acted like I hadn't called him earlier. I asked him if he got my phone call. He said, "Yes." I asked him if he listened to the voicemail. He said, "Yes," again. I asked him why he didn't call me back. He said nothing. I wanted so bad to lash out, but with my sister's words still fresh, I didn't. I had to trust her, and trust God, and the only way I could do that was to be quiet. So that's what we were, quiet. He had stopped talking, while I had to learn how to hold my tongue.

I continued to talk to my sister for the next few weeks and months; and she continued encouraging me to listen, to use my words, to not confront, to write everything down, but most of all, to pray. I'm not going to say that I wasn't praying for my husband before, but I wasn't praying for him like I should have been. Because during this time, my prayer changed—not, "Lord, change my husband," but "Lord, change me. Even if that means I have to accept that this is the way my husband is going to be for the rest of our lives, Lord, change me to accept it." I hated that thought, but that's what I understood needed to happen. I had to change, not him. I couldn't even think about the moods, or the bipolar depression, I had to change just to get through the day. I had to change, because my conditioned response was to imagine cutting my wrists and letting him feel the guilt but wondering if he would even act. I didn't even know if he loved me anymore. And while we had both said that divorce was NEVER an option, I had to wonder if that's the path we were headed towards. It got to the point that even the kids noticed his silence.

I continued praying. I continued journaling—this was an encouragement I was getting from all sides: my doctor, my sister, and now God. It felt like he kept telling me that I NEEDED to write everything down. I didn't understand, but I obeyed. In the midst of that, God and I started having conversations. It wasn't just me talking, or complaining, but us conversing. I would write how I was feeling (though I knew God knew) and then I would read his word and see something in there that was applicable to my life. And as much as my life was a disaster, I discovered I could find a little respite from it in my time with God.

There was much I learned, but early on, he told me I didn't need Mo's permission to love him. You see, I had come to the point where

I didn't know what to do with Mo—did I respond to him as he was responding to me? Not out of spite, but out of a sense of respect, to give him his space to deal with whatever he was dealing with. But that felt like it was taking air out of my lungs. I didn't know how I could do that, or how long I was supposed to wait before I showed him love. But then God told me I could love him whether he responded to me or requited the love. I could still say, "I love you." I could show him that love, I could do for him what was in my heart to do because of the love I felt for him.

And so, I did. It felt good to be able to express that, but it was also disheartening because Mo did not respond to me. But I continued doing it, I continued being quiet and showing him my love.

The day for my surgery arrived—February 14, 2017. We never celebrated Valentine's Day because Mo felt that it was a commercial holiday, and he said he didn't need one day to show me his love. But in my mind, that argument was moot, because I felt like his love was something he barely showed on the other 364 days. But I had to remind myself that even if he didn't show it, I could. So, I ignored his silence and talked to him like we did in the past. They prepped me for surgery, and while my words were fewer now, I was still determined to show love.

I woke up several hours later, the surgery a success, with only four small scars to show for it. I was eventually taken to a room. There was a chair to my right, and a bench by the door. Mo chose the bench by the door. My son and daughter came to visit, talk, and hang out, but my husband still said nothing. Eventually, they left; and it was just me and him. He looked at me and asked if I was okay. I said, "Yes," then he said he was going home. I told him that was fine. I was expecting to be discharged by about noon the following day and I would see him then. I chose not to think about him after he left.

The following day, he waited for me to call him before he came to pick me up, then he brought me home. He had cooked for me and helped me get in bed. But he slept on the couch that night, and while I understood that he was giving me my space, I couldn't help the tears that flowed. Even with the care he was showing me, I felt alone.

I healed and returned to work a couple of weeks later. I started trying harder at not being negative, not being angry. I was still having mood swings, but I had again determined to not show that part of me to him so as not to give him an excuse to pull further away. I knew damage had been done already, but I didn't know what else to do to fix it. I continued journaling, even breaking away during my day to talk to God. When things got rough, when my emotions got the best of me, that was all I could do to get myself under control. I continued praying, "God change me." I continued showing love without waiting for permission to do so. I was texting him now in the mornings, just quick messages saying, "I love you," or wishing him a great day. But he never responded to any of them. I was trying, but the situation felt like I had already lost him.

THE WARNING

MAURICE: Up until this time, I've only had two sovereign God-moments concerning Ruth. The first was when I was dragging my feet on marrying her and God gave me a glimpse of my life without her. That is the only time where I actually thought living a life without who God had for me would not be worth living. I had no intentions of ever harming myself but that was my 'scared straight' moment. The other time is the one I mentioned earlier, right after we got married and God told me that I had better honor the special covenant he has with her. Years later, I was about to get the third moment. I believe it was the summer of 2018; it was a hot summer day and like times past, I was at work driving along thinking about her, and on the issues I thought she had. I remember hearing this: "YOU KNOW YOUR WIFE IS A GOOD WOMAN."

This seems like a simple statement, but what I heard (and saw) was, "What you see as negative someone else would love to have." One thing I know for certain is this: if God was saying it, there would be no more open doors once it was shut. This was early in the morning and I could not shake that feeling all day. It was a feeling actually that lingered for weeks. Sometimes it would lay low and other times it be a jolting that would just shake me to the core. All the outcomes of this would be negative if I didn't change. I couldn't sulk or drag my feet anymore. So, first things first, I would have to tell her exactly how I felt. I remember it was a Saturday in that same summertime. I don't know if we were having a disagreement or not seeing eye-to-eye. I was sitting on the edge of the bed in our room, sharing my heart with my wife. I shared the anger and the pessimism, and how that led to the fact that I actually didn't like talking to her. I shared how I felt that we couldn't have a real conversation without tears or emotions. I also asked her what or who she was angry at because I felt she was angry at something or someone (which, again, might be me).

The look on her face was shock and tears (which is understandable because I had just given her a lot). I don't remember all the details of the conversation, but I do remember her looking at me and telling me not to hold my feelings back like that anymore, no matter how it might hurt her.

Her comment shocked me, and I knew I should have opened my mouth a while back. In a very strange way, I felt a little relieved; I didn't have to hold back anything. I could just focus on communicating better.

The other thing I learned is this: even though you may not say anything, your spouse can usually sense when things are out of rhythm.

RUTH: I was sporadic at first, but I continued showing Mo my love. At one point, I spent two weeks texting him, but like before, I got no response. One morning, I struggled with doing it. Not because I didn't want to, but because I doubted that day would be the day he'd respond. I was at work, and not feeling hopeless, but not feeling hopeful either. And I remember it was as if God said to me, "Don't worry about him, just spend time with me." So, I did. I took a break, pulled out my journal, and started writing. This became our mode of operation, even as Mo and I continued the way we were.

After a while, though, I started seeing changes in my husband, small ones. Mo would ask me questions now. He would flirt with me. His answers were becoming multi-syllabic. The conversation was still minimal, but it was coming back.

Then, about six months into the year, I received a text from him.

> *I know you have said it a bunch of times in text with no response from me. But I never want you to doubt, wonder or even entertain the devil's thoughts on this.*
>
> *I love you back, the good, the bad, the right, the wrong, the anger, the crazy & all that's in between. Yep all of it.*
>
> *You have my back & support me. I don't say this braggingly, you are crazy about me. I think sometimes my presence gives you oxygen. That's a special place to have in someone's heart.*

It's an honor & a privilege to be there. Trust me God is holding me accountable.

I recently realized that we have grown & mended together, so to be separated would be a tearing from you which would HURT.

Never wonder, I ♥ you. I cannot stop...nor want too!

I was at work, going back and forth between my desk and the reception area and only caught part of it. When I was finally able to read it, I started crying. It was an answered prayer, but it was also more than that. Mo's wording wasn't accidental or thoughtless. God was holding him accountable, and he was showing me how much he loved me. He was working out our marriage, mending it.

That text served an additional purpose: it was something I could go back to when the doubt crept in. When the silence overtook us. When I became anxious and overwhelmed. I could look back at it and know that my husband loved me, that God still loved me and was looking out for me. This wasn't the 'and-we-lived-happily-ever-after' part of the story; but it was the beginning of our healing, in more than one way. And that's the important part because I started to see that God could heal … even me.

Mo was still working through whatever it was he was working through. Part of me wanted to ask him, but I knew I couldn't, I knew he wouldn't respond. So, I continued to stay quiet, continued doing what I was doing—journaling, seeking God, trying to control my moods. But I continued having issues because I had no emotional intelligence. That's when you're mature enough to control your emotions, to manage yourself. You condition your mind to be strong and build your tolerance to take more. I didn't have any of that. But I now understood I didn't, and I became earnest about seeking and going after God.

But it felt like I was on a seesaw—up one moment and making progress, down the next and losing ground. I didn't change on the outside, I was still that same person battling with bipolar depression, battling with suicidal thoughts, battling with sharing myself again with my husband, but I was trying. I was battling the battle and trying to keep the ground I made. We were both trying.

One morning. Mo sat me down to talk to me. I didn't remember that until I read his entry. But as I took in the words, I recalled sitting on the bed, hearing his heart. I was hurt, and I cried. But I listened and, in the end, asked him not to hold back anymore.

We were both slowly breaking through the walls we had built, but you have to understand, like everything else, when you do something long enough, it is now your conditioned response. I was emotional and often out of control, while my husband was reserved and often stoic. We were headed towards healing, but we still had hurdles.

I kept writing down my goals, but I was failing in that respect, especially the daily goals. I knew I had to track my moods, but I still resisted. I was lazy. I didn't want to do this every day. I didn't see the point in it. But I knew in my heart that's what God was telling me to do. So, I determined in my heart that was what I was going to do.

Then an episode hit. It was a Sunday morning; I was supposed to serve in children's church. But the depression was so debilitating, I didn't know what to do to pull myself out of it. I am a morning person, so I got up early to get ready. But the longer I was up, the longer the moods had to consume me. And that's how I felt, consumed. I knew God's word, I knew this was temporary, but I couldn't see beyond the nose on my face. I tried not to cry, not to feel so hopeless, not to give in, but there was nothing left in me. I had to wait for Mo to wake up to talk to him, but even as I waited, there was a war in me. I wouldn't have talked to him if I thought I could handle it, but I couldn't, not anymore. My moods were dropping and the only thought that was clear was the one encouraging me to cut open my wrist.

At the same time, I was afraid that by saying something to Mo, it would change how he acted towards me, it would diminish the progress we had made. And that he would judge me. He would say what he always said: "Why don't you snap out of it? Why don't you pray? Why are you telling me?"

I had to time it. I couldn't talk to him when he woke up—he didn't have enough time for that. I couldn't talk to him when we got home from church because he had errands to run. If I talked in the car, I knew he wouldn't respond, because he'd feel like I was ambushing him. I'd be left feeling alone. And feeling alone was worse than feeling the depression. So, I talked to him as he got ready, and he responded as he always did:

"Yes…but why are you still dealing with this? You don't want healing bad enough. You're comfortable with this. It's your crutch."

I was devastated. I tried arguing, tried explaining, but he didn't listen. I couldn't stop crying. I texted the children's church director and told her I couldn't serve. She didn't ask, didn't argue. I would talk to her later and she would tell me that she understood something was wrong—that she had seen me starting to pull away and knew I was starting an episode. That she was praying for me. But I didn't know that now. I only knew that I was alone. I had no one.

The tears continued throughout service. Then an altar call was made. I went up, and just cried. The intercessor who prayed with me stayed with me the whole time I was up there, standing, then kneeling, on the floor, then on the chairs. We were there about twenty to twenty-five minutes. Everyone else who had come up for prayer had gone but she stuck with me. She repeated what my pastor said to me: "It's always darkest before the dawn, Ruth."

Dawn was coming, but right then and there, I was in my darkest place.

The tears eventually stopped. I felt spent. But I also felt embarrassed. I felt like all eyes were on me. Like everyone knew. But that day was the final straw. I had broken down in front of my church, but it was the catalyst that pushed me finally to change.

The next day I started charting my moods. I couldn't find one that fit what I was trying to do, so I created one. The tracking itself didn't change anything, but by my next episode, I started seeing patterns. I would wake up with the depression, and that would set the mood for the day. What if before I allowed the depression to set my mood, I set my day by focusing on God instead? This wasn't a one-and-done deal, but it was something I could do, something I could practice. I started changing my diet to fit my needs. I hated going to the gym, but I could walk. Eventually, I would start running, which I discovered was something I enjoyed. The mood swings continued, but as I kept up with the chart, as I started changing my words, as I started making lifestyle changes, I began to see that healing was possible. I didn't share what I was doing with anyone, mainly because this was now my mode of operation, but I was beginning to see change. I was beginning to see the light at the end of the tunnel.

WHY

MAURICE: Whenever you go through something, there is always a 'why' as to the reason for it. Sometimes it's not a simple cut-and-dry answer. Life is a journey and God is showing you things along the way. It was an early fall morning in 2018 and I was heading out of town for a work assignment. I received a call from a close family member who simply wanted to complain about nothing and wanted me to do something I was not in a position or willing to do. I remember getting off the phone and being very disheartened, disappointed, and slightly frustrated at my family member's actions. So much so that I had threw my hands up at the whole situation. I had a full day at work, so the job consumed my time and energy which was good.

The next morning, I had to travel to another city, and because of the distant between the two cities, I had to leave early in the morning (a few hours before sunrise). I'm always pleasantly surprised at how quiet and clear the early mornings can be. As I drove down the highway, I started thinking about the phone conversation I had the day before. The feeling of frustration and disappointment returned. I remember almost saying I definitely needed help because I truly had no answer. I didn't know where to start, or even what to do. At that moment God begin to speak, not necessarily about that situation, but he said:

"Do you know what depression is? It's like being in a room or in a place that is as dark as what you see outside"—I was driving down the highway in a rural area at that moment—"It's so dark that you can't see your hand in front of you, even though you know it's there. That dark place never goes away, and after a while, a pain from that darkness develops. It's nothing sharp but it is a gnawing feeling that never dulls. The reality is this occurs on the inside, so no one sees it. Even though you look okay, a person with depression is far from it. The average person won't recognize signs of a person dealing with depression, as most people with depression get good at hiding it. What's even more frustrating to a person who is dealing with depression is that they see all the normal things and people who are around them and the only thing they want to do is be like that. But they have this darkness and gnawing constant pain."

He gave me the example of being underneath a house in the crawl space.

"It could be a bright sunny day," he said, "But when the door to the crawl space opens, it's very dark. If you go in and close the door you can hear the world around you, but you see nothing except a darkness that's inescapable. People who live like this are silent screamers. They scream, 'I'M HURTING HERE, DON'T YOU SEE ME? DOESN'T ANYBODY CARE?' That is because they live where I just described. The only time you really see the depression is usually when it's too late, when they act out what the world thinks is an insane action but it's simply the inside manifesting on the outside. This is something that you cannot just take a pill for or do a mental exercise for a while and it's cured. It first takes understanding the issue to even begin to help someone with it.

"This is what your wife has walked through. Even though she had a family, she's had to walk through it alone. And because she has had to walk through this by herself, she knows that pain and has a keen awareness of this type of pain. She has the ability to look at people and see this pain and darkness. Her words as she speaks will carry weight that when she says them, they will cut through everything and minister and help people who are in the 'crawl space of pain' in their life. People dealing with depression will know she is for real because her words and actions will speak directly to them."

At this point, I began to talk audibly, pretending Ruth was in the car. The difference was this time instead of telling her what was wrong with her, I began speaking life into her. I also saw her on a stage, talking to a crowd of people. I heard the Lord say, "There will be people Ruth will see, she won't say anything to them, she will just give them a hug, and in that hug will be a crack in the dark place they are in. It will be like someone opening that crawl space door on a bright sunny day while they are sitting in the dark crawl space. It won't light up the whole area, but it will be enough for them to see there is hope and this will give them a path to move towards."

As we were speaking (God speaking to me as I pretended to speak to Ruth like she was there in the vehicle with me), my eyes began to water a little as I realized that even though we were married, Ruth had truly done this alone. In that moment, I saw the strength of this small Puerto Rican woman I had married. She had strength I knew I didn't, and I marveled at it. I truly believe, at that moment, she was not only my wife but a heroic person as well.

But I also thought, "God, why are you telling me this? After my actions, I don't deserve her love."

These thoughts consumed me for a few days. I thought about our paths into the worlds: one of us almost wasn't born and the other arrived slightly damaged, but God knew and had a plan. He had something in mind we didn't see.

I also thought about my career path. I've worked in the media for almost two and a half decades. I've seen a lot of things and met a lot of people. I've seen hundreds of people speak from presidents to governors to CEO's and everything in between, so I have heard a lot of good and bad speeches. I have been in a lot of rooms that I might not have had the privilege to be in otherwise, so I had an understanding of what works and what doesn't. In that moment, my career began to make sense: the knowledge I gained in my time in television was to help my wife in fulfilling her purpose.

When I see things like that, I like to talk them out. A few days after I saw that, I was in my work vehicle driving, talking out what God had revealed to me and it hit me! My career path was not for me, but for Ruth. I must say I almost lost control of my emotions. After all I failed to do, and all God had to do to get me to see the true courage, strength, and beauty of my wife, he still wanted to use me to help her. The thought of that excited me and my heart instantly said, "YES!"

Life is a journey of seasons; the beauty of it is being able to live long enough to enjoy them. They don't always feel good, but they all have purpose. I think the greatest fulfillment is taking the time to understand them and the gift is being allowed enough time to figure them out and help others along your path.

I don't know the final outcome of the path I'm currently on, but I feel it's a purpose that God has given me. Do I know the details of where God will take Ruth and how many people she will speak to? No. I just feel my career has led me to the path to be her support so she can help those who are in the dark.

I'll end it with a sport metaphor: even if a player on a team doesn't play in the championship game, if they are on the team and their team wins, they all get rings. I'm excited to simply be on the team, even if I'm just support from the bench. Because the ring is coming!

RUTH: I was several months into this new process, into my healing, still experiencing mood changes, now seeing that it was possible for me to heal. My husband and I were leaving a class at church midweek when I was approached by a church member. She asked to speak with me and proceeded to tell me her daughter was struggling with mental illness and didn't see the point of even going to a doctor and getting a diagnosis. She started to ask for advice but requested instead that I would speak with her daughter. I said yes. I didn't know what I was going to say and certainly wasn't even sure the daughter, who was about eighteen years old, would even speak to me as her mother had dragged her to church just to get her out of the house, but I was willing to help in whatever capacity I could.

The daughter and I found an empty room and spoke for about an hour. I shared with her my story from diagnosis to present-day and what God had done for me. And she shared her struggles and her hopelessness. We were able to connect in a way that she couldn't with her own family because I understood what she was going through; and even though I was only in the beginning of my healing, she could see beyond the hopelessness. She told me at the end that this was the first time she had heard anyone speak about mental illness and God and not get weirded out by it. I laughed, but I also encouraged her to get a diagnosis and start her own path to healing. She said she would;

and her mother eventually let me know that she did.

I left church feeling high. That sounds perhaps wrong, but I understood then that a purpose could be applied to the pain I had endured. I understood that for everything I went through, someone else could benefit from it. Someone else could find healing.

And indeed, that's what I was finding. I continued tracking my moods. I now saw that I was cycling every two months for two weeks. I could now 'predict' when my depression would hit, and I could be ready for it. I learned the difference between internal (biological) triggers and external (non-biological) triggers. I learned that I was conditioned to respond in certain ways and that by understanding what set me off, I could now change how I was responding. I learned that bipolar is more than feelings and moods—it is also physical symptoms: fatigue, tiredness, nausea, pain, etc. I also now understood why I ate so much around my episodes: I would get tired and being desperate for energy, I would eat food, hoping to find it there. All I found was eighty extra pounds, because then my body was conditioned to eat out of habit. And that's what most of this boiled down to—habits, conditioning. I behaved and responded a certain way because I had done it for so long. And because I didn't realize what I was doing, I just kept doing it.

When my kids were growing up, I would often tell them, "If you don't know why you do something, don't do it." The same was true here. I had to relearn how to eat, how to exercise, how to respond emotionally because I didn't know why I was doing what I was doing. I had to learn that emotions were not something to be afraid of or to ignore—they were a gift from God, given to help us. Mine were unbalanced because of the disease, and the resulting response, but even in this, I could learn how to feel again, and how to feel correctly.

As of this writing, the progress I've made on the inside, can now be seen on the outside. My healing is not just limited to my mental health—I am in the process of becoming whole. I have lost eighty-one pounds and reached my weight-loss goal. I have gone from a size sixteen to a size six. I run every day, not just to keep the weight down, but because I enjoy it. I am off of medication, but I've had to discipline myself in order to do that. I no longer respond to ninety-five percent of what used to trigger me (I think I'm stuck with the last five percent simply because I am human). I'm learning how to deal with the cycle that still happens every two months for two weeks. I no longer respond emotionally, like I used to, but I am learning to deal with the physical symptoms that still affect me to some degree. I no longer have suicidal thoughts or idealize death, though those thoughts pop up every once in a while. We are all still a work in progress. None of us will ever reach perfection, but we can experience progress and I've done that, progressing from quitting, and wanting to die, to living free from emotional instability.

In all this, God's word remains true.

> *No temptation has overtaken you except what is common to humanity. God is faithful, and He will not allow you to be tempted beyond what you are able, but with the temptation He will also provide a way of escape so that you are able to bear it. 1 Corinthians 10:13*

The word temptation can also be translated as affliction. So, whatever your affliction, whatever you're going through, God has a way out, he has an escape out of that situation for you. You just have to go to him, you have to believe in him, because he believes in you. I heard those words in the 2002 film, 'The Count of Monte Christo' and they have stuck with me ever since. Even through the tough times, when I didn't believe in God, he still called to me, still encouraged me, still believed that I could do the very things that would bring me peace and healing. Even when I was pushing him away, denying his power and ability, he was waiting for me with a plan. But I had to come to the point where I could hear him so he could share it with me. And I'm not going to lie and tell you it was easy—it wasn't. There were times when it seemed easier to go back to the way things were, but I kept pushing. I developed discipline in many areas, I had to learn about myself, which, if you read the introduction, you know that feat scared me more than living with this disease. I also had to humble myself, I had to admit my mistakes, I had to apologize, I had to ask for help. I had to dream again. But the end result was worth it. I am the epitome of, 'If I can do it, you can too.' And I'm here to tell you, you can.

I will not say, if you do what I did, you'll get the same results. We all have our own processes: my walk is different than yours. But the principle remains the same: God has a way out for all of us. My way out may look different than yours, but the 'out' is something we can all experience.

PURPOSE

MAURICE: I read the book 'Millionaire Success Habits' by Dean Graziosi. One of the chapters in the book talked about the seven 'why's': you ask 'why' and for every answer you get, you ask 'why' again. You repeat the process seven times, going deeper each time. Ever since reading that, I've found myself asking and even trying to answer the 'why's' in my life, especially when I don't understand something.

So why did I write this book? The answer for me is simple: my Christian faith has caused me to develop and have a growing love for people and a desire to see them love, succeed, and overcome. One of my answers to 'why' is that I feel we (mankind) can do better, and this is how I can help achieve it. In our fast paced, instant gratification society we can easily fall into the 'me, myself and I', right-now mindset until something so intense happens that we have to stop and address it. Sometimes when we have addressed it, we move on (sadly back to the self-focus mindset). But there's always more when life challenges/crises arise. They not only affects the person(s) who's directly facing it but will most likely touch those who are connected to that person(s) with the challenges/crises.

This book was designed to hopefully make you stop and think that there could be others who are indirectly connected but intimately affected by our actions. Often in life, we make mistakes, but for whatever reason, we have a hard time acknowledging them and sharing them with others. My hope is that in sharing mine, you can avoid the pitfalls I fell into and you can get to your destiny and fulfill your purpose quicker than I did.

I pray my 'WHY' will help!

RUTH: At some point near the end of 2019, I had the thought of asking Mo what happened years earlier that made him stop talking to me. But I decided against it. I trusted God and if I never found out, I was okay with that. I loved my husband tremendously and that is enough.

Then Mo sent me the manuscript for this book, his portion of it. I think part of him was afraid of what I would think of him (*yes, very true. –Maurice*), now knowing what those years truly were. But here's the thing: when I first read it, the most immediate thought wasn't hurt over what he admitted, but "Did I change?" I wanted to be sure I wasn't that person anymore. In general, but especially with him. I cried later when I reread it, now absorbing the truth of the situation, but I could still only see that he was human and there was nothing I could hold against him without seeing the guilt in me. Not the fabricated shame that became habit over the years, but the true guilt, the guilt of sin. There are times I feel I need to apologize for words I said, or actions I took, but I now understand that my change is my penance. As long as I'm applying what I've learned, as long as I'm living the truth of God's word, I will never have to say, "I'm sorry" again.

That is a powerful motivator. I started writing by sharing about the shame I felt in telling my story. There are words and actions I can't take back, years I wasted. But the truth is, the past does matter. I may not have liked what I went through, and I would never choose to willfully repeat it, but I now understand that memories are essential for future thought. They help us imagine and project ourselves into a future that is yet undecided. We may have had happy memories, or they might be miserable ones—both help us envision a future, where we search for the happiness we knew or seek to never repeat the misery we experienced. When we deny or block our memories, we blind ourselves to what could be. It's painful sometimes to think about them, but if you will allow God to walk you through them, you'll find the place to mourn what you need to mourn and the place to heal where you need to heal.

Ultimately, that is my 'why', my purpose, in this: to help others see that healing is possible. Not just with mental illness, but with life in general. When God does things, he doesn't do them half-way. If he is offering healing, it's for the whole person. He isn't saying, "I want you to be healed in one area." He's saying, "I want you to be whole in all areas. I want you to be whole in your mind, your body and your soul."

I hope to eventually share my process with a wider audience, but until then, I continue moving forward, living my life like I am a light on a hill. I'll be the example for others, so that they can know God has a way out for everyone, if you're only willing to trust him. It's not an overnight process, but if you will hang on, you'll discover a journey worth taking.

MORE INFORMATION

To read more about mental illness, visit the following websites:

- National Alliance on Mental Illness (NAMI): www.nami.org
- Mental Health: www.mentalhealth.gov
- Substance Abuse and Mental Health Services Administration: www.samhsa.gov

If you or someone you know is struggling with depression, you can text 'Go' to the Crisis Text Line at 741-741. It's free and confidential; and someone is available to talk to you 24/7. Visit their website at www.crisistextline.org for more information. You can also call the National Suicide Prevention Lifeline (800-273-8255) or NAMI (800-950-6264) for support and local referrals.

ACKNOWLEDGEMENTS

MAURICE: Ruth Griffin, you are a rock star! You truly have a purpose, so much so you enter the world on your own terms. People with great struggles usually have great purpose...ma'am that's you! There is purpose in your pain! You are stronger than you'll ever know. I marvel at it. I look at you as a gift God gave me...in no way I deserved. I believe when you look back over your life, you will be amazed at who you've touched and what you did. I love you is not enough but that is all I can say...you have no idea how much and there is not enough time in the universe to show you (insert my tears here).

Bishop Godbee, thank you for loving God, your family, and The River the way you do. In those simple actions, you've spoken sermons (even when I knew I was wrong) to me that touched my life and the Griffin's forever.

If you ask me what legacy is, the easiest, most meaningful way for me to show you, is simply show you a picture of five people. Irence Crawford, Thomas Sr. and Dannie Griffin (grandparents), Ruth Griffin and Bishop Ronald L Godbee. They may not be super famous or known on multiple platforms. Trust me those who they've touched, they have influenced will forever (and beyond their own lives).

RUTH: Mo, if I am a rock star, then you are my rock. I wouldn't have made it as far as I have without you, and I look forward to where we're going to go. Now we are truly walking together, and though the road has been lined with pain, heartache and yes, anger, I have no regrets, because it's brought us to where we are. I love you more than words can express. I still believe we were made for each other, and this journey has only solidified that. Thank you for taking the initiative and writing this book, I'm happy to be your completion.

Javin, Hannah and Samantha, your love has been unconditional, even when I was at my worst. Thank you.

Onette, Jackie, Victoria, and Andrea, you are the true definition of a friend, and I appreciate you more and more each day. You listened, you advised, you encouraged, you loved. And I wouldn't be where I am without you. Thank you.

ABOUT THE AUTHORS

There are two types of people in life: those who express words better verbally and those who express words better written. Maurice L. Griffin is the former. It showed early on in his life—as a B/C student in English, he did what he had to do to get through school and college. But he knew the importance of communication (words can create and or take life, along with everything in between). So much so that this was his major in college—no, not the written form, but verbal expression, studying and eventually starting a career in media. This verbal form has kept him employed for over twenty-five years as a television photographer at a local news station. When Maurice is not shooting video and interviewing people though, you can find him either exercising at his local gym, or in the kitchen cooking for his family. From the latter was born a passion to create his own barbecue sauce: a sweet, tomato-based, 'Kansas City Style' barbecue sauce called Jena's BBQ & Baked Bean Sauce. Jena's is currently available online and in few specialty stores in the Raleigh-Durham, North Carolina area. A Michigan native, Maurice has been married to Ruth for over 22 years. They reside in North Carolina and have four adult children.

Ruth E. Griffin began telling stories at a young age, first with pictures, then with words. Even though she always considered herself an artist first, Ruth has been writing since grade school. She penned her first book as a teenager and has continued writing since then. Ruth is now the award-winning author of several books, which center on women's experiences. She is the founder of Studio Griffin, LLC., a full-service vanity press that offers publishing, graphic design and writing services; as well as a cohost of Authors Up, a streaming radio show that provides a platform for new, established, and aspiring authors. A New Jersey native, Ruth now resides in North Carolina with her husband. They are parents to four adult children. Her books are available at all major online bookstores.

www.ingramcontent.com/pod-product-compliance
Lightning Source LLC
Chambersburg PA
CBHW021427070526
44577CB00001B/94